Stirred Oceans

Poetry to stir your soul

Molly

notionpress
.com

INDIA · SINGAPORE · MALAYSIA

CONTENTS

ABOUT THE AUTHOR

Born and raised in Uttar Pradesh of India, Molly is an aspiring poet and writer. Growing up she was always fascinated by literature and this interest led her into the world of writing in the later years of her graduation.

By profession a teacher, she got bachelorette degree in science and did masters in english to satisfy both of her urges. Introverted by nature She is a lover of naps, poetries, long walks, sky gazing and music.

Molly who writes under a pen name, In her writings explores varying human emotions. From social issues to personal growth and from love to nature, She is an avid advocator of self-help and self-love.

You can find her on both instagram and facebook by simply visiting her artist account under the handle name "stirred_oceans_".

May you feel both

the calm and little unrest

As that's what Poetries do the best.

STIRRED OCEAN

Opposite poles of the magnet same.

One rests in the north.

The other is in the south.

Quiet eyes with the laughter loud.

Encompassing a calmed soul

As well as a nosy heart.

Her mind; A battlefield.

Her bod; A shrine.

With the rings of fire

along its depths.

She is an ocean

that's at outburst.

POETRY AND STORY

DEATH AND POETRY

Verses more often than not,
are born at the end point.
A broken yet beautiful
aftermath of the breakpoint.

With twinkling hazel eyes
under the serene sky Roman
and the heart's beautiful
condolence to a dream broken.

A sudden outburst of
the thorn laced flower
in the quiet moments
of the untroubled hours.

A gateway between the
realms virtual and real.
The chosen residence on
the basis of human ideals.

POESY TANG

Fragrance of the soul unknown
starts dripping down when off
the foramina of the soma.
Know that; it's the poetry
that's been birthing its aroma.

It's a bod made of emotions
afloat in which are the words.
A fuel transported throughout
It's life support for the life force.

STORIES

Every minute and every second
born are stories so many
some of which live for a jiffy
while another for an eternity.

Story of a baby's laughter
and the dilemma thereafter.
About a snowflakes birth
and it's union with earth.

The sound of the quails returning;
grateful for surviving the killing.
The tales about prying of guilty
and then the defying of the silly.

About the wanderer who never left
and the residents who flew to the west.
Truth behind the sore in man's voice
and the prideful glimpse of rejoice.

The dream of building some small town
where happiness never falls down.
And the fear crawling in the big cities
filled with ambitious disease.

About how the past with unforgetful blues
creates the present with positive views.
Fables of the myth and the truth
Some forgotten while some in azimuth.

These are the stories.
Some big, some small.
These are the anecdotes.
Tales new and old.

EMPOWERMENT

ADVERSITY TO EASE

The dark black pit residences
in alleys darker than darkness
are not the places seen just by you
as it's where everyone once has been to.

It's where dwells the monsters in the pool
seen alongside whom are the angels too.
Memories created then subsided
it's all in there side by side.

Being that's submerged in the subconscious
still surfaces to peek out of the dungeons.
Playing since birth different roles
it's your own blood, flesh and soul.

Hence embrace it all no matter what
for it's all your existence's part.
At the end of which awaits the orchard
that is full of your hard work's reward.

BATTLEFIELD

After a life time spent in the darkness
some end up missing the beacon of hope
they like a chick inside an egg
hence are unable to break through.

There they'd stay still; awaiting as if
for the death's embrace; unaware of the fact
that breaking through the cocoon is
the only option a butterfly can ever have.

Dark even if is a mother's womb
still when the life prevails
tearing it's way through
sliding here it comes.

That's how is the fate
called which's the life
born in the battlefield;
That's where we'll all die.

BATTLES INSANE: LIFE

In this game called 'Life' that's so insane

don't you fear crossing the 'Lanes'.

May be dance with the devils

and play all those games.

Don't you remember?

how the battlefields were never

meant for the 'Sanes'.

BLACK N' WHITE WORLD

In a world divided into sides two

enemies are easily found midst blue.

Truth where comes wrapped in varying hues

lies are much easier there for people to brew.

With dichotomous thinking and behavior skew

the detrimental acrimony is destined to sprew.

Consistently diminishing gratitude and respect

while take place often in such cruel conduct.

The divine presence of an unusual rebellion nit

or a mere glimpse of the humanity's sudden grit

is all that's needed to hold the altruism torch a lit.'

LAYERS OF A WOMAN

She is the vessel incarnated who's as a creature

the one who carries the euphony of nature.

Inner core whose made of mighty sea

treasures are found there in deep.

N' Before you doubt her light don't forget

of the balancing element from the hell

along with enough fire on the outer shell.

Mantle is the home to the mother earth

for she is the source of every birth

And the holy land of thine cultivation.

While crust is the wide blue yonder

where dreams often take the flight

battling fiercely the inner fight.

Such is the prominence of a patroness

Who has been begotten to be wondrous.

INNER STRENGTHS

When in darkness;

Do you extinguish the flickering candle?

For the fear of its running out anytime.

When it rains;

Do you leave the umbrella at home?

For the fear of its getting wet.

When faced with the storms;

Do you confide yourself in a corner?

For the fear of these winds hitting strong.

NO.

Never.

Not at all.

You lit up a new candle;

When the first one runs out.

You leave the umbrella under the sun;

to get it dry again.

You still go out fighting the winds

N' winning over the storms.

Don't you?

Then what does stop you

from stitching the torn parts.

Getting up n' Growing.

Loving fiercely.

all the while living freely.

LIVE TO WIN

Battling it's way out of the mother's womb
you who came out into this world to bloom.
What is it that you fear?
Can it be the pain you might need to bear?

Sure enough at times the world is cruel
but who stands it all is the one to rule.
Precisely that's why in the long run;
The first thing is to pick our preference.

As All the difference is made by those who fought
while living the life they thought they ought.
So is it scraped knees or the handicapped leg?
Or fearing blood spilled while climbing the crag.

For how else can you reach home?
when on the necropolis of
the never lived possibilities
throughout your life you roam.

So live to win.

Even with the guts spilling

N' the scar that's still aching.

As living is the never ceasing struggles

Filled with the varying unpredictables.

For what is death?

but to be surviving somehow

with the long gone soul now.

METAMORPHOSIS

The youngest and the most vibrant

and also who's gorgeously fragrant.

Engrave this in thy mind;

those filthy hands so fiendish

will never be able to demolish

thy bona fide psyche

that burns so bright.

Neither can they rob you off it's beauty

for you're the manifestation of a deity.

Rather they will carry thy fragrance

unable to shake off your substance.

Mighty alpine child;

no matter how strong the storm

never will it be able to shake

your hurricaneous spirit

and that herculean grit.

For those who effectuated you to break

will forever be unaware of the fact

They've created the most exquisite mosaic.

METTLESOME PERSONAGE

When thy life turns into
a tough row to hoe;

Remember this

We're the offsprings of the queen
bracing who is this planet green.
And fruits of the vigorous king
gifted by whom we are all with
the soul drenching, sprinkling.
With our souls so incredibly firm
and our hearts home to the griffin.

When life seems like
the walk on the ropes.

Don't forget
that's exactly what it takes
to be the sky to
someone's ground of hopes.

MOON CHILD

No matter the darkness how deep;

I could still dive out with light indeed.

For the sun in me would never ever cease

while the warrior me can't care any least.

Since the truth isn't arbitrary,

And I'm the moon child with

the moon inside my territory.

Hence come forward my dear

for the treat

N' I promise that's where

we will meet.

UNCONSCIOUS SALVAGERS

Far beyond the cumulus cloud
a sacred kingdom can be found.
Dwells where the immortal soul
captivated by diversified roles.

Sleeping who's in the dark chest
needs to be awoken from the rest.
For on the other side of this mirror
we're all our own fairy godmother.

The parallel universe,
it's name other
where the victim is
its own savior.

UNFOLDING DESTINY

Halt take a step back and
discover all that you lack.
Let the sun peek through the knobs
scatter and caress these hair-locks.
Stretch the hand under pouring clouds
come out of your self-indulgent moulds.

Let the winds brush off this skin
drip into it the bod brightly sheen.
You see the door is still unbolted.
Owning to thy hope that's upholding
While The pandora's box was unfolding.

And there is still a
long way left till shore
For there is a lot more
in the time's store.

VICTORY

The tears your soul once bled
will wash your path of all crud.
While the never ending struggles
one day will vanish into bubbles.

The lifelong yearning for the grace
will see the rise in its embrace.
While the scar lands of battles lost
will bloom into the richest orchard.

And with it; the page turner fortune
will unfold into the colossal boon.
Where the infinity will echoe a roar
when the cosmos welcomes you to soar.

VICTOR'S ODYSSEY

We are the pawns however not so same

in a life that's said to be a game.

Where each one is entertaining the other

for savoring almost the same pleasures

while taking all the necessary measures.

.

As like in the game of snake and ladder

stepping the ladder;surpassing the other

Just to be swamped n' thrown to the bottom later.

.

Or probably like in the chess

wherein the mighty your highness

won't wink before ceding pawns

for the so-called bigger plans.

.

Or maybe like in the game of carrom

where the queen is the most pitiful one

her life is on stake twenty four-seven

at the hand of some striker random.

Yet in any event; the only conviction
in this wild carnival is the proposition
that there's a winner for every tourney
who at the end completes the journey.

WARZONES

After life long dancing around the clock
you still find yourself behind the lock.
As Lost as the keys amongst the variables
that always ruin the long setup tables.

I know nothing seems to go as planned
And you end up tip toeing in mine lands.
Maybe that's why valor is our life jacket
The only key to the victory in this combat.

For when life seems to be a treadmill
there is no way you can stand still.

NATURE'S CHILD

While outfacing the nature
and carrying the essence
of the wild flowers
patent who's in all its glory.
You are the weed who still
grows defying all the calamity.

Carrying the depths of the pacific
as ancient as the age paleolithic
with the untamable soul monolithic.
Oh Nature's fledgling favorite!
You aren't a fairytale that's mythic
but a lifetime journal that's explicit.

Carrying who's within
the infinite celestial beauty
you're an expanding galaxy
of the constellations
with whose warmth n' light
the stars get emblazon.

Carrying the magma of

the burning mountains

And the river to

the nature's profound fountains

you're the sun out of which

Life transpirings.

THE AMAZON

She; the bud in blooming;

with a mouth full of spikes.

Pierces the existence of every

hand aiming towards her psyche.

She; the hopelessly hopeful

is the guardian of the soft in the harsh.

Inside whom resides decades of autumn

still awaiting for the spring without end.

She; the savior of her own

with monsoon as her companion

prevails again n' again

and takes the crown.

WHY?

When the waves are wild

and the winds are strong.

Why look for the shade?

when Gaea trembles with thy roar

a banyan tree reaching its core.

.

With the night getting dark

and lightning hitting hard.

Why fear the sky being a little crazy?

Did you forget that the sun rises

even when the sky is hazy.

.

when the doors have been locked

and they don't answer the knock.

Why just sit around in vain and yelp?

when your awakened soul is there to help.

FEARS

COMPATIBILITY

A Lifelong search for
a relation harmonious
is a self-imposed
hardship that's onerous.

Since for you even
a camaraderie that's commodious
is a puzzle that when falls out
is nothing but erroneous.

They ask you to pick a way
that's not querimonious
without pondering over
its trail that's loneliness.

Though how do you reach
an agreement with fire
which knows nothing
but to overtake and ignite?

DEPENDENCE

An army of ants
lined up, undeviating
tracing the one ahead.
Prick just one.
Trembles the rest.

A flock of birds
returning home at dusk.
A soaring pattern
of the diminishing dots.

A herd of sheep
headed towards the aim same
irrelevant of the fact
whether it's going to be
The boon or the bane.

A four chamber villa
with space tight
Unfortunately is the
residence to life.

GROWING UP

Looking at the adults all around.

The struggles they got to face.

The struggle they finally tamed.

N' the struggle still awaiting them.

The cruelty of the wild burning world.

The lack of humanity

N' the stash of antipathy.

Seeing this constant state of weariness.

The newly grown up child wants to tarry

a bit more on the threshold of adolescence.

EFFORTS

When a force extrinsic
goes above and beyond
somehow too late it's
before the truth finally dawns.

Results then it only into
a toil on the very bod
supposed which was to be
able to move abroad.

For vital no matter how much is
the satisfaction of the receiver
important no less is
the capacity of the container.

So tell me,

On the scale of 1 to 5

How does one measure

the merit of saplings fruitless?

And what possibly can represent

the defaulter's progress?

INFREQUENT BASEMENTS

The noises in the basement below
falls dead on meeting the steps slow.
The light doesn't brush their heads
and they lay there since long unfed.

The air seems to have not been through
guarding maybe someone was the windows.
Having grown comfortable under the candles
some things resist the summer sun's opulence.

When the rusted key and dusty knob
join the hands to unbolt the lock.
You shouldn't leave them untouched
for it's the time they are washed.

NOSTALGIA

An unbidden visitor
knocks the door for formality.
As unpredictable as it's stay
it reoccurs for the mockery.

In the dead of the darkness
would sneak under our blanket
to rest it's weight on our chest
Curling the toe with heavy breath.

Night seems long under its presence
and we sing to it all our secrets.
Saltwater flows breaking the dams
with acceptance as its aftermath.

The moon being sacred witness
and silence the only friend.
Nights might be the ends
but mornings are the genesis.

With this drill

we think of dying

just to be born anew

the next spring time.

PAIN

He,she, you, they and me.

None of us here is its grasp free.

Doesn't matter whether it's

a mother awaiting her fallen son

or a woman anticipating

her perished husband's return.

For they both go through

the ordeals equivalent.

When "click" came the sound

on striking the palms

leaving afterwards it's mark

on both hands.

What steps did you take to differ

one shade from the other

whilst they both had the same mother?

The only difference marked

is in the way it's expressed

and how it comes to the surface.

While comforting;

maybe it's easier to compare

suggesting how so many

have suffered the unfair.

Though how helpful

can be that consolation

which enters with

an extreme expectation?

So keeping it all aside

the truth is

No matter what's

the hue of the pain

it irrespectively

hurts just the same.

REGRETS

Shadows knocking on the door
or the ghost beneath the floor.
No matter where you run
they'll find you to shunt.

The foxes under your skin moan
for the life that's on the loan.
Hiding away all the grim of your face
waiting for the reaper at the end of the race.

You take the account books off the rack
wondering why the balance sheet won't match.
At last looking back for the first time
you sit there alone counting the dime.

TO BE THIS OR THAT

Under the possibilities

meager and governed;

The world tells thee

to choose either this or that.

And with demarcation as such;

He still tries his best.

He tries to be this

for the sake of his

and that for thy ease.

Having pretzeled chords cardinal

to fit in thy successive ordinals.

He subliminally time and again

gone keys would try to regain.

WISHFUL NEWTONS

Even though they know,
"The World is not a wish granting well".
they keep throwing in a coin still and all.
Being a sentinel there then;
they wait for it to come true
Somehow in the end.

Given the human tendency
of wishing then forgetting.
Slogging through the tracks
with a mind ever changing.
Wondering about the destination
Whilst walking in the daydream.

Ignorant of the power of gravity
which their hard work carries.
Sleepwalking they spend day after day
while waiting for that one heyday
when the apple would fall down their skull
giving the world their brand new conqueror.

WORN ON HOURS

Sleeping soundly to the beating now
while running on the times ticking hand.
Did you catch the train to the morrow?

Ignorant of the seasons changing
family turning; their backs vanishing.
Did you not hear the futurity knocking?

Running out of breath on life's treadmill.
Did you catch up on the lost yet precious miles?

Does the turning ghost of today
not suffocate you to sleep?
Or did you decide not to visit the graveyards
of the smiles lost with the moments glowing
Where life flourishes to a still beating heart?

Tell me is it you running out of time
Or is the time running out of you?

LIFE LESSONS

BALANCE

No matter how much
the empathy looks lovely,
Forever can't be applied
to the elements worldly.

For the things eventually
loose their original shapes
when mixed they are
into the varying shades.

Although aware we're
of water's importance.
The fact is; even it can
kill with its abundance.

Hence balance is the only
key to the safe zone.
For too much of anything
just crushes the bone.

ERSTWHILE TILLAGE

Obviously a rotten harvest
can only be cultivated
when the foregone memories
yet again get mistreated.

Since asinine it is to keep on
mistaking it for our scarland
that in real was nothing else
but the hallowed farmland.
Sown in where were
the seeds of the present
the key to our being
a prosperous merchant.

So better learn to respect
and love it all the same
as it's that holly domain
contributed which has to
the present you possess
while constructing
the future you'll access.

LETTING GO

When holding on
isn't plain sailing,
letting go doesn't
symbolize failing.

As it's what we're
practicing since birth,
in exchange of the absolute
peace on the earth.

Sometimes the only way
for starting anew
is letting go of the
cruelty aiming at you.

While holding onto the pieces
going towards their ruin
which in actual fact is
called cherishing your fortune.

MEDICINE

The door that seemed

to be forever unlocked,

closes which on our face

as we now pull the knob.

'Tis there to give us

the taste of our own medicine,

on behalf of the times

we too didn't see n' listen.

And perhaps this all is

a part of the test,

which reminds us of the things

we shouldn't ignore at our very best.

MUTUAL CONCESSION

In this era

of give and take;

where real can no longer

be cultivated with the seeds fake.

Where the feelings

hurt are proportional

to the intensity of

the havoc self induced.

Forgiving is no option

in the karma's menus.

Hence the only path then left

is this worthful present;

laid here since forever n more

for a future that's in store.

For even with the animal

who's tamed under the fear
knows only how to come around
just to bark n' bite its owner.
While nourished when the same
is with the affection
sacrifices he makes
to cure all the affliction.

REAL WISDOM

Since the Wisdom comes here

not with just observing

while strolling in the

absence of understanding.

And Just how a plant can't

grow well in a cemented alley

For it needs to be

cared for in a fertile valley.

Needed much more is of the one

who dreams of being called

the true quick witted.

With every bit of the experience

absorbed into each of his neuron

rushing through his linked veins.

He too has to be a being that strong.

As in this world real

he has to be prepared

for the kinds of hardship

he would need to bear.

STAGE OF AFFECTION

When the fruition of the
coveted is well deserved,
blooming of the red camellia
with it is then observed.
As the efforts made
to keep the acquired
has exceeded the endeavor
of what was desired.

Whereas confronted when it's
with the self acclaimed unfair
promptly disappear then
it all into the thin air.
For when the things are
finally taken for granted
there is no way for it to
turn out how you wanted.

UNFORTUNATE TIES

While people come only for later on to go
holding on is the only thing we would know.
As if our life is a door with a broken knob
with people who know nothing but how to rob.

And we the foolish know nothing but to give
breaking at every exit as we go on to live.
Learning the lessons hard as we move on
forgetting what we already learnt head-on.

But sometimes forgetting is also a bliss
as you cut off the snakes that still hiss.

SELF DISCOVERY

COLORFUL TEARS

What feelings are real and do really count?
Are they the ones that are obvious n' renowned?

Based on the color that water puts on
when from the eyes it's trickling down;
Would it become easier for thoughts to disown
if this way the emotions can be trailed down?

With purple giving off the empathy
n' yellow emitting the sunshine warmth.
Where orange represents a sense of security
and green ensures the faith and calm.

If red warned you about the upcoming danger
and blue told you to behold and be cautious.
while black being the evidence of the grief.
would it all then reassure your lost belief?

DISAPPOINTMENT

How do you see it?

A dismayed feeling of the lost hopes

or a beginning point for new scopes?

What would you want?

a proof of a human heart full of emotions

or a four compartment hard rock devoid of affections?

What is more disappointing?

getting to taste it again n again

or never taking a chance because you're scared of pain?

What is fortunate?

to be the ground for someone's expectations

or being left alone with shallow relations?

LONE HOURS

Long delayed hangover
of the good old times
instigates which the
self deceiving crimes.

In the dead gray hours
of the silence
a feeling that creeps
into the lense.

Clouding all the
self imposed reasons
attempts it the theft
of the alliance.

As no underlying desire
can forever be suppressed
When the attempts of
self-restraint gets messed.

Hence forever ignored

psyche's instant conquest

is observed more often

in the moments of unrest.

A KINGDOM OF MY OWN

For years;

I have collected the words unbosomed

on the creases of the eloquent tomes.

And have catched the fallen leaves of

the old oak trees on my way back home,

after picking up the rose petals in the

backyards of the garden cities of Rome.

While watching stars and the moon that's

tracing the stardust on path that gleams

with the inner child's igniting dreams,

I have engulfed the cold winter breeze

and drank drizzles off the heavy heaven

amongst the hymns of birds and the bees.

And years after,

These words have become mine remedy

in restoring the astraying humanity.

The leaves I caught have taken me on rides
at the back of the gentle breeze to look
at the dreamland I'd seen in some book.
And those rose petals still have their scent
lingering on my palms which later I've had mixed
into whatever I had done and wherever I went.

The cold breeze has turned my bod as strong
as the roots of a hundred years old banyan tree
which grows in my grandma's porch wild and free.
The raindrops still cleanses me inside and out
while keeping off the muddy touch of the world
which on my untouched soul might act as mould.

The moon's lightening my path on darkest of night
while the stars have given me dreams to shine
as I carry the stardust in my footsteps
used that's to trace me in my own wonderland
which after all these turmoil finally I got to set.

THE BOTTOM LINE

Wearing a rare bod to fulfill duties

which's home to everchanging beauties

with its forever revealing mysteries.

Without being subjected to worldly liabilities,

based just on its restricted sight of vicinities

how long can one truly strive for the affinities

In the world extended to infinities?

.

Bearing in the mind world's outlook freaky

and how the warmth turns into bergs icy

whenever the situation becomes dicey.

Wouldn't even the strongest psyche

stumble and turn out to be flighty?

then in a world as such,

How far can one go onto duck?

THE LIE AND THE TRUTH

A castle built on the foundation of illusions.

Worth measured by the alien mouth's voicing appreciation.

A cosplay well chosen or a self-deceiving delusion.

The never ending hoops of forever ongoing invasion.

An unwelcome series of corrupted thought's intrusion.

A fate to be sealed based on the much needed exclusions.

A black hole with an end but ending into only diffusion.

A path ending at a crossroad and the upcoming confusion.

A chance served to all and a call for the final decision.

A venom sweet or an elixir bitter? Turning in the conclusion.

An inevitable future in the lap of time that is hidden.

A fallen looser's grave or the unwavering hero risen.

THE RIGHT ANSWER

For the underlying questions and the scars,
in a world with as many answers as the stars.
How often do you go through the hansards
searching for those desired right answers?

Tell me how much gray do you see
in between the right and wrong,
And where do you belong?

Inside the same room but at opposite hem
between the right you and the wrong them.
When do the actual battles begin?

And to know the absolute truth and it's relief,
How often do you keep in check your belief?

THE UNCONSCIOUS

When a room full of windows

with thoughts as the passerby

becomes the fiery pit

where it all sinks down deep

into the abyss of the mortal domain

where till eternity it shall remain.

Some will still be imprinted

on this immortal existence

with others being evaporated

into the mere diffidence.

That's when it's awakened in you

with the lighthouse soul

while helping you sort the way out

to climb high n' have a better view.

THAT RIGHT RIDE

You may feel like home
when you stay long
though doesn't staying lone
makes it bore even more?

as the subway you chose
might bring you home
but if it's crowded
won't it make you suffocate
with you dying at the gate?

Hence; try to board the train
reserved one n' only for you.
And it's absolutely fine
if you change the line
when it didn't fulfill its due.

For to embrace
you the whole,
there're many more
already on board.

COEXISTENCE

Wandering no matter where are you and I
Dwellers we are under the same blue sky.
Never do we escape vagabond winds embrace
No matter which direction you and I face.

By far quenched our thirsts are from the same well
And the air you exhale fills the life in me as well.
Wearing our bods might be the hues unlike
But made we all are of the elements alike.

So diversity among us can't be put to blame
For we are the colors of the rainbow same.

SOCIAL EVILS

BLOODSTOCK HUMANS

Humans abandoning humans
for selfish reasons
have forgotten what is it
to live like one.

Having born as the race horse
wearing the blinkers as a mask.
Startled by the noises slightest
the trivial clouding momentous.

For the reasons obscure,
running we've been towards
the directions unvarying.

We beings as such, reared
in the hands of society
are the marionette
suffocating humanity.

REGRESSING HUMANITY

The epitome of

patience and lenity

whenever is mistreated

n' taken as levity

resulting out of

the lack of sanity

can mark just the

fall of humanity.

For every women

in this world

even after being a

living-water mate;

doesn't qualify any ogres

to quench its thirst

as they do with

the butter n' bread.

DISCRIMINANTS

Personas of diverse hues
habitats of planet blue.
Breathing the same breeze
claim to be of elite breed.

Oblivious to the fact that
the lord has made them
of the elements very same.
Ignorant fools go on to
tear it into the fragments.

Coward murderers of the brave
later end up with unrest
in their own grave.
Hiding face behind the flick
It's a generation who is sick.

Even so fortunately,
once in a while

Goddess Gaea births

the gems as peeps

who after all this

still won't reek.

FORCE

It might all seem to work the same way

whether turning coal into the diamond

or the matter into the black gold.

Surely with push takes birth the blessed

while the door opens with the piston pressed.

Though arises also with it the sick delusion

when taught since elementary is the youth

force is necessary for the things to move.

Hence encouraging the thoughts vicious

that pressure only ensures the precious.

Forgetting pressure does also bring forth

the sea of larva with long time suppression

and the angry tsunami in response to larceny

of the solitude and the solace of the calm sea.

HYPOCRISY

Black is the sky at full moon's night
the hue in the absence of the light.
Preference in terms of coffee
the eyes and hair for so many
except when it covers the body.

Free birds they all dream of to be
breaking the chains they try to flee.
Though freedom comes here with a price.
No wonder not everyone here keeps pride.

Easy here is not the life of any maiden
She is the home to the secrets hidden.
Her fate is being the root of the family tree
bearing the fruits while seeing the birds flee
She isn't granted even the weekends leave.

You think the whole world is unfair
when you aren't offered your share.

You who never descended the stair
with an empty stomach and feet bare.
Have you ever seen the kids in the rag?
If not then you know nothing about lack.

Fascinating it's to throw pebbles in the lakes
giggling at the ripples it afterwards makes.
Surely everything seems fun and game
until it's you under the conditions same.
Though shame not over your hypocrisy
for some things can't be changed
even through long term literacy.

IMPATIENT IGNORANTS

So many of us want to read
others as a book that's free
completely blindfolded towards
the value it might carry.

Many here wish for a
feast that's totally free
ignoring the indigestion
they may clearly foresee.

Many would let go of the
rope unaware of the fact
that they're halfway into
the destination's flat.

And many here would
look for the easy rides
not knowing these hardships
lead to the secure heights.

Impatience hence

standing out a mile

runs in their veins like

some diluted water deficient

of that very basic ingredient.

LUXURIES VS HOME

High buildings all
decorated in glaze
still wanderers are left
straying with no place.

In warm attics
with basements cold
is where stays
buried their souls.

As it's the home nowadays
that's the biggest luxuries
for the ones who've
turned into the escapees.

PLASTER SAINT

When respect doesn't the man other beings auxiliary

but rather worships instead the invisible visionary

is exactly when misery comes in the way of sanctuary.

Mounting his high horse down he treads the high track

just to come down backsliding in the face of the crag.

Treading on the heels of echo in the pied piper's grave old

"Disrespect the entity and worship the power which it holds".

Blaming the dead moving forward under the conscience tipsy.

The plaster saint has made peace with the time old misogyny.

POLITICS

When self interest stands
against the very humanity
begins then the game of
the terrifying insanity.
As the desire to stand
atop a league neverending
brings forth often the
consequences beyond mending.

A black hole like reason
those who go on to own
care not for the manchineel
they have long grown.
A generation thriving like
an egg plant on a plate
programmed that's been to
specifically bite every bait.

Living like a pawn placed

on the checkerboard

who is constrained to

follow the laid down road,

is precisely the reason

for the understated wrong

where the ultimate vision

has been long foregone.

RISE OF THE REBEL

'Man is the master of his own destiny',
they said.
Wasn't it clearly a caution
that centuries ago relayed?

Then why ignorant of the facts
man still plays dirty
thinking these games will
pay off the rewards worthy.

Not knowing the real
essense n' message behind,
he interprets and bends
the words to suit his kind.

Consequently leaving
no other resort possible
but only the anticipated
dawning in the rebel.

For has everyone

lived a life decent

there won't be

any mates to resent.

And has everyone fought

a fair and square fight;

we won't really be in the want of

reformers to set the society right.

RULES

How do you think the generations
before us were ended?
Could it have been when towards
the cruelty humanity was projected?

How do you think the doom day
would have then started?
Oh! shouldn't the human's
contribution be complimented?

A great society on the heap
of rules which is founded
How come the injustice there
then had been accepted?

N' What could it be that makes
even the law corrupted?
Is it a greed tainted heart
that no longer can be melted?

A pack of wolves in judiciary

at tribunals well educated

knows best how to make use

of the self conscience rusted.

But then again how could

the ruling be questioned?

when need of the moment

that's frequently amended

is often the only set of

obligation that's assented.

SALVATION AN ILLUSION

Assuming the death as the fated end
hopefully an unwary life you won't spend.
And although fake has been in trend
hopefully towards it you didn't wend.

For eternally broken things can't be mend
by using the time at the end which is lent.
On facing evil whom would you dare depend
when while alive only cruelty you defend.

As leaving all dirt you dream to ascend
with gratitude you think you'd be sent?
But what if at the end of the tunnel
there awaits you yet another scuffle.

SNOWPLOW PARENTING

Wrapped up in the silk cocoon

after years n' years of blindness

imposed by the afraid maiden;

when the blindfold falls down

the world to her child

seems further more turbulent.

For the drops collected in the sea

when knocked off brings the tsunami.

And havoc is nothing but

the self induced forces of

the past deeds taking shape

of everything you try to bury.

BIRTH OF MONSTERS

Monsters are destined to be born
in the world of give and take
where often the return is late.
Turning into the lack of vehemence
given people's fathomless ignorance.

Forgetful of fertilizers being implemented
while misusing the time that's been rented.
Shunning everything that the bygones meant,
they'd wait for the harvest festival's advent.

As if dwelling forever in the dark
ever granted a key out of the lark.
Without a letter where being taught
with light forbidden to be brought.

THE ENDLESS GREED

In a world set on the trail to destruction;

Nothing can parallel the mind's corruption.

Where monsters reside in every nook,

hidden beneath the facade with no dispute.

When the multitude slowly turn into the vulture

preying who's to appease it's incessant hunger

with the imprisonment of the senses offshore,

serves it then as the root cause for the uproar.

THE GOLD BIRD

Snapping; Breaking; Adjusting

in the pockets and the grip.

With the people out on stake

In the world as such

regardless of their taste

roaming hungrily every alley

to take down things as many.

Be that Gold bird;

needed which is to be held with

the marrow of their existence.

THE PROCESS

There is so much to protect and guard
so that the self-esteem isn't jarred.
In a world where more often than not
when the curtains are not pulled off,
The effort is looked down upon and laughed.

While in the midst of echoes of applause,
it's tossed and crushed as a mere luck.
Extinguishing thus the sparks inner
ergo resulting in more losers than winners.
Unconscious of the blood that's been bled
the fool asks for the proof of the sweat shed.

For how many do really see the track
leaving aside the prizes of the rack?

WARS

Somewhere desire for prestige

leads to the birth of the racist.

While aiming for the top of pyramid

in this journey soon your rides

initiate using others as sidekicks.

Man turning into the brainless activist

forgets the obligation of a humanist.

Where in the battle of foolish ambitions

suffocated is the least ounce of reasons.

Terrifying is the sight of wars inside and out

for black swallows all the colors no doubt.

Who can blame the law that's blind itself

when no-one seems to care for line meant

to separate the guilty from the innocent.

Irony dances often on the face of peace

as finally discrimination seems to cease

When youngsters; woman; child n' oldsters

are seated in a room full of the accusers.

Who here is qualified to pass the verdict?

When all we know is just how to predict.

WORLDLY MANACLES

Not knowing better the foolish blunders

while the society is playing the hunter.

And in this process so unpredictable

Society's poison births the blisters.

We being the energies recycled since forever

which neither can be created nor be destroyed

hence end up expanding and contracting in the void.

Feminine; Masculine or Neuter

What exactly is the soul's gender?

May be if was known to earthlings

would have prevented all the flings.

Showing exit to this circus rings

leading only to what doesn't stings.

Alas! it's not the world that fair

as even born fortunate suffers in here.

DREAMER

BEING SOFT

In this lavish worldwide play
being the hunter and a prey.
Fulfilling a life span in a food web.
Surviving we're in the giant colosseum
by the rules of the wilderness.

A santient paradigm of the
gentle, pretty and pure.
Why can't one strive to be
a swan,lamb or a honeybee?

Within an incessant battle
of the ecosystems
ignorants aim of reaching
the pyramid's top;
when the riches were
hidden at the hub.

Living a tiring,unhappy

and a lonesome life;

Why do they dream of

being a lion while alive?

Daybreak's sunshine

after a frosty night,

what's wrong with

being a soft psyche?

DAREDEVILS

May be you climb up the mountains

just for the suicidal bunjee jump.

Probably you dive deep into the oceans

just only to drown yourself to death.

May be you pass through the doors

soughting to be left shut inside.

And you fall deep down just to be

soaked into one of the black holes.

For the every "BE CAUTIOUS" sign

triggers the beast inside of you.

And you run in to play with the fire.

Precisely that's why they can't stand

this gold plated sight.

DAYDREAMERS

DREAM.
Even if it's an impossible dream.

Go on and wish.

Wish on the shooting stars.
Wish upon the meteors.
Wish while blowing out the candles.
And Wish with the eyes n' ears closed.

But don't forget to
DREAM with eyes open.

For you never know;
which dreamland you
might end up flying off to.
And you never know;
when it'll all come true.

FATE SEALED

Born are the humans with the tag
no matter whether a lass or a lad.
With the obligations of being a progeny
carrying are they all the laid prophecies.

Paths that were supposed to be discovered
often are the only options that were served.
For the inforced destinies at every crossroad
eventually make the determination fall short.

As taught we are all to be worthy of others
from parents to the spouse then the children.
Cosplaying we take the birth then die the same.
Never giving the thought about what we are
or caring for the real you, me, us and all.

Hence not knowing their inner wealth

many remain enclosed in the destiny's shell.

Though once in a while; you still see the brave;

with the bloody knuckles who wrote his fate.

They are the sailors of the self-discovery

the living paradigm of immense bravery.

GAMBLES

I hope the only gamble

you will ever dare to bid

would be the one where

into the uncertainty

Eventually;

reality will slip.

HERCULEAN SOULS

Obstinately determined and challenging.
An ardent heart without a trace of flinching.

Bearing who's the ocean's profundity
in addition to the flower's delicacy.

A heart which can't be defeated by destiny
Standing tall; it's the almighty's progeny.

HURRICANES

Sweet lies set afloat on the horizon

stirs the mind's cauldron into crimson hues

when the helios is set off to his home.

All tangled up are the signs beyond reasons

and the heart falls prey to the hunters mesh.

While tempting is the predator's bait;

rescuing the prey is often too late.

But here is the thing about the gentle winds

with the derived force; hurricanes it brings.

Hence when hunting hold tight on to your grounds

for whom you mistook for someone weak and fragile

might as well happen to sweep you off your bounds.

INSIDE A FANTASIST'S PHANTOM

What do you call it when

fake delivers the absolute.

Emerges when it from

the shadows taking forms real?

Do we call it pretense

when clutched is life essence

in the trickery brimming

that's with raw emotions?

Ask an aesthetic anima

of the beauty it observes

in this unconventional

n' mystically cryptic orb.

It'll open then the portals

Of the realms unheard n' unseen

Of mirages seen amidst the oceans

and the islands in the oasis.

Of how the strings of her marrow

have pulled in her psyche

making it dance to the rhythm

of obscure yet true emotions.

MIRAGE

When thoughts are provoked down deep
and memory lane turns up to seep
the moisture out of thy tongue
In the midst of the vast wilderness
Beautiful daydreams are born then.

Igniting a beacon of desire deep within
escorting thee out of the long labyrinth.
Leaving a bittersweet taste behind
and a hankering for some more in sight.

RETURN OF THE WARRIORS

The praise that gives way to the new openings.

The lightning that enlightens the ignorants.

The hurt that awakens the sleeping beasts.

The healing that caresses the angel's wings.

One day the oceans resting beneath stirs

flooding the soul while breaking the curse.

Which is how the universe expands

welcoming warriors with acclaims.

STELLAR

Blinded by the light

at the end of the tunnel,

we are the stars chasing after

another star in an empty funnel.

The stellar practicing

the art of astronomy.

Embracing the star dust of the millions

of the galaxies sprinkled upto infinity.

He's that earth dweller

who's yet to be aware

of the core elements

of his unearthly ambience.

TENACITY

Patience; they tell you to have
as if it'll suffice what we lack.
Thinking karma is watching our side
the weaker ones tiptoe their whole life.

Dancing on the fingertips of fate;
They wonder why the fruit is late.
But it's rebel who doesn't take the bait
and with his passion the heavens shake.

THE GALLANT REBEL

We are all mad, we've always been

admirably imperfect human beings.

When you say right, we'd go to the left.

In an intruding society we dare theft.

N' when the life sets us on it's cruel test

we come out to hunt it down with our best.

For we rule the world with our own spells

fate bows before whom; we're those rebels.

VAGABOND SOULS

For thee who always seems to ponder

n' crosses thy path with some wonder.

It's not the negligence of thy mind

as gypsy hearts indeed aren't easy to find.

And there aren't really many who are set on

to be seen soaring into the wild blue yonder.

Yet confined can't be the vagabond souls

by the mortal's terrestrial boundaries

as their mind explores the deepest seas.

WARRIOR'S SPIRIT

The sailors sent by the kingdom
of my head had always given in to
the storms in the oceans of my heart.
And the frequent fire in the forest of
my life has time and again returned as
an ash by the extinguisher of my soul.

While being heedful of the twitching
in the womb of future; giving away
which is the signs of the days ahead.
Life keeps advancing no matter what.
For the struggle is not over yet
and the battlefield is ever ready
for us; the warriors to be met.

Nevertheless welcomed it's all here
for this bod is forever ready to
take off with the spring break breeze
and a pair of the wide spread wings
into the infinity to own whatever it is.

WISH GRANTING WELL

The world might not be

a wish granting well.

But only for those

who are too lazy

to throw the bucket in

and too afraid of spilling

their guts in getting it out.

GLOSSARY

A

Abroad - in different directions; over a wide area

Acrimony - ill feeling

Advent - arrival of a notable thing

Alpine child - Exhibiting characteristics of a high mountain; expressive; optimistic; inspiring

Altruism - unselfish concern for other people's happiness and welfare.

Amazon - a member of a legendary race of female warriors.

Anecdotes - short amusing stories about real incidents.

Anima - the soul, especially that irrational part of soul that differs from rational mind

Arbitrary - based on random choice or personal whim

Asinine - extremely foolish

Auxiliary - an additional helper

Azimuth - the direction of a celestial object from the observer

B

Begotten - brought into existence

Black hole - a region of spacetime where gravity is so strong that nothing can escape it

Blinkers - a pair of small leather screens attached to a horse's bridle to prevent it

seeing sideways and behind and being startled; something which

prevents someone from gaining a full understanding of a situation.

Bod - body

C

Cardinal - of the great importance; fundamental

Ceding - giving up

Colossal - huge

Colosseum - a large theater, cinema or stadium

Commodious - roomy and comfortable

Conviction - state of being free from doubts

Cosplay - practice of dressing up as a character from a film, book or game

Coveted - greatly desired

Crag - a steep or rugged cliff

Crud - substance which is considered unpleasant

Cryptic - mysterious

Cumulus - clouds forming rounded masses heaped on each other

about a flat base at fairly low altitude

D

Demarcation - action of fixing the boundaries or limit of something

Detrimental - harmful

Dicey - uncertain; unpredictable

Dichotomous thinking - the tendency to think in terms of polar opposites—that is, in terms of the best and worst—without accepting the possibilities that lie between these two extremes

Diffidence - modesty or shyness resulting from a lack of self confidence

Domain - kingdom; empire

Drill - intensive instruction in something typically by means of repeated exercise

E

Effectuate - put into force or operation

Elixir - magical or medicinal potion

Emblazon - illuminate

Endeavor - earnest prolonged effort

Epitome - a person or thing that is a perfect example of particular quality or type

Erstwhile - past; old; former

Euphony - quality of being pleasing to the ear

Explicit - stated clearly and in detail leaving no room for confusion or doubt

Exquisite - extremely beautiful

F

Fantasist - a creator of fantasies

Fathomless - immeasurable; endless

Fiendish - extremely cruel

Fledgling - baby bird

Flings - a short period of wild behavior

Four compartment hard rock - heart that has become hard as rock

Futurity - A future event, the future time

G

Gaea - the Greek Earth goddess; Mother Earth

Gallant - brave; charmingly attentive

Genesis - beginning

Griffin - A mythical creature with the head and wings of an eagle and the body of a lion who represents the wealth of the sun. The griffin symbol in Christian art represented strength, invincibility, watchfulness, and the relationship between psychic and cosmic forces.

Grit - courage and resolve

H

Hallowed - made holly; greatly honored

Hansards - official records of debates in few countries parliament

Helios - the God of sun in Greek mythology

Hoe - to weed, cultivate with a hoe (a long-handled gardening tool)

I

Incessant - continuing without pause

J

Jarred - shaken

Jiffy - a very short time

K

Knob - a rounded lump at the end of a door to open or close it

L

Lad - a boy

Larceny - theft

Lark - something done for fun; an activity regarded as foolish or waste of time

Lass - a girl

Lenity - the quality being kind

Levity - light-heartedness

M

Manacles - handcuffs; restraint

Manchineel - a tree that's famous for poisonous fruits

Marionette - a Puppet worked by strings

Meager - very small in amount

Mettlesome - full of spirit and courage

Misogyny - dislike or contempt for or ingrained prejudice against women

Momentous - of great importance

Monolithic - powerful, indivisible and slow to change

Morrow - the following day; the near future

Mosaic - a picture produced by arranging together small pieces

Myth - a widely held but false belief or idea

N

Necropolis - graveyard

N' - abbreviation for and

Nit - used as a warning that someone is approaching

O

Odyssey - journey

Ogres - a monster

Onerous - troublesome

Opulence - richness

Orb - globe; the earth

Ordeal - a very unpleasant and prolonged experience

Ordinal - a number such as 1st, 2nd….. that shows the position of something

P

Paleolithic age - old stone age

Pandora's box - a process that once begun generates many complicated problems. Pandora's box is an artifact in Greek mythology

Paradigm - a model; an ideal

Patent - easily recognizable

Patroness - a woman who protects and supports

Personage - a person of great importance

Phantom - something existing only in imagination

Pied piper - one who offers strong but delusive enticement

Plaster saint - a person who makes a show of being without moral faults or human weakness, especially in a hypocritical way.

Pretzeled - twist and bend

Profundity - wisdom

Progeny - offspring

Prominence - importance

Prophecy - a prediction of what will happen in future

Proposition - a statement that expresses a judgment

Prying - excessive interest in person's private affairs

Psyche - human soul, mind or spirit

Q

Quail - a small, brown bird that is shot for sport or food.

Querimonious - prone to complaints

R

Reaper - short for grim reaper (personification of death)

Red camellia - a kind of flower that symbolizes passion and deep desire

S

Salt water - tears

Salvager - someone who saves something from danger

Sentinel - a soldier or guard whose job is to stand and keep watch

Shunt - push or pull from the main line to a siding

Sidekick - a person's assistant or close associate who has less authority than that person

Skew - suddenly change direction or position

Slogging - walk or move with difficulty

Snowplow parenting - parenting in which a person constantly forces obstacles out of their kids paths

Soma - the body

Sprew - to pour or send forth with force or violence in large quantity

Stash - store safely in a hidden or secret place

Still and all - even so; nevertheless

Subliminally - unconsciously; subconsciously

Swamped - overwhelmed with an excessive amount of something

T

Tarry - linger; pause; wait

Tenacity - mental or moral strength to resist opposition or danger

Threshold - starting point

Tillage - land under cultivation

Times ticking hand - clock

Tomes - a book, especially a large heavy scholarly one

Tourney - a tournament

Transpiring - occur; happen

U

Unbidden - uninvited

Unbolted - opened by drawing back a bolt

V

Valor - bravery

Vehemence - passion; spirit; enthusiasm

Venom - poison

Vigorous - strong, healthy and full of energy

W

Wide blue yonder - sky

Wondrous - inspiring a feeling of wonder or delight

Y

Yelp - sharp cry of pain

Yonder - the far distance;

ABOUT THE BOOK

(SYNOPSIS)

The book contains poems written in different styles on varying topics and emotions. From social issues to personal growth all find a place in this masterpiece.

Each poem here comes from the depth of the being which, like an ocean when stirred for long, produces all kinds of valuables awakening the conscious and subconscious thoughts within and makes us ponder.

So yes,

Grab it now if you too are habitual of daydreaming and questioning both the self and Whatever surrounds this self.